The fact about : Deer

CB

The fact about: Deer
Copyright © 2022 Cara Bea
All rights reserved. This book and its images may not be reproduced or used in any manner without the written permission from the author.

Deer live in places like wetlands, forests, rainforests, grasslands and mountains.

They are herbivores
meaning they eat things like plants.

Deer love to eat grasses, the leaves off shrubs, herbs, mosses and fruits.

There are 60 different types of deer in the world.

A male deer is called a buck but the larger and strongest male deer are called stags, a female is called a doe and baby is called a fawn.

Only male deer have antlers except for the species of deer called Reindeer the females also grow antlers.

Each year their antlers fall off and grow back.

There is one type of deer that do not have antlers, even the males, they are called the Chinese water deer.

Deer live all over the world except for Antartica, they did not originally live in Australia but have been introduced a long time ago in the early 1800s.

Male deer will lock their antlers together when fighting.

Deer can jump very high.

They are also very good swimmers.

They keep their noses wet by liking [licking] them,
this helps their sense of smell,
being able to smell a predator from far away.

Their eyes are on the side of
their head which gives them wide vision.

Deer have excellent night vision as they can see Ultraviolet Light. This helps them find food and keep safe from predators at night in the dark.

Deer love to travel in groups called herds.

When baby deer 'Fawn' are born they have white spots these disappear as they grow older.

In the snowy winter they use their hooves to uncover leaves or moss.

Deer have the best hearing, they can hear you if you make the slightest move.

The only domesticated deer is the reindeer.
This means that they live beside humans.
They are very friendly animals.

Deer like to rest in a safe place like under a low hanging tree branch.

Other books

The fact about: Bunnies
The fact about: Pandas
The fact about: Triceratops
The fact about: Honey bees
The fact about: Koalas

Printed in Great Britain
by Amazon